WHISPERS FROM WITHIN

WHISPERS FROM WITHIN

DANNI KELLY

Whispers from Within copyright 2024 Danni Kelly.

All rights reserved.
This book or any portion thereof may not be
reproduced or used in any manner whatsoever
without the express written permission of the
publisher.

ISBN: 978-I-7637327-0-4

Front cover image: openart.ai

First printing edition, 2024

Danni Kelly
@_danni_kelly_

for summer, steele & luna

whispers

SECTION 1 - TRANSFORMATION (1 - 31)

SECTION 2 - MOTHERHOOD (32 - 50)

SECTION 3 - SONS & DAUGHTERS (51 - 77)

SECTION 4 - PARENTING (78 - 97)

SECTION 5 - LOVE (98 - 104)

SECTION 6 - SIMPLE BEAUTY (105 - 115)

SECTION 7 - THE PATH TO HERE AND NOW (116 - 118)

Section I

TRANSFORMATION

don't put me in a box
all my life
i've been jumping out of boxes

| TRANSFORMATION

what if it's not words
that will inspire others
but seeing us
the ones of us that choose it
dancing and playing
in our sovereignty
in a realm without fear
let's go
beyond right and wrong as Rumi says
i'll meet you there

| TRANSFORMATION

she peeled back all the layers
until she was bone dry out of excuses
now it was time to step into
who it really was
she came here to be

| TRANSFORMATION

we sit peacefully within the cage
somewhat enjoying being hand fed
all that we think we need
completely unaware
of the shackles that contain us
blissfully and obliviously
content

until one day
our eyes open wide enough
to see a bird fly past
and we ponder
what am I missing

and that one question is how it starts
followed by an avalanche of a thousand more

and we grow
and we grow
until the walls start to cave in on us
and staying where we are becomes unbearable
so we overcome our doubts
and we build up our self belief
and then one day, we find ourselves
flying

and before long
we're flying outside of the walls
of someone else' cage
and our wings are softly whispering

come fly with us,
come fly with us too

| TRANSFORMATION

whisper something
really kind to yourself
right now

| TRANSFORMATION

clumsily
she stepped off the-merry go-round
like a small child
learning to walk
seeing everything with fresh eyes
holding a knowingness that every thought
from here on in
would create the world around her

and so she thought of love vaster than the ocean
she thought of the type of joy that makes your cheekbones ache
she thought of traveling to italy
with only two intentions
pasta and wine
and she thought of every human experiencing the gift of living life
with presence

her world had changed
she had changed

like a fairy's footstep
or a flower's petal
her, her life
and everything in it
had become delicate

she was comfortable in the stillness
and in the stillness
she wrote
and she wrote and she wrote
and she danced and she sang

and the words on the paper kept this world alive
and the words on the paper kept her alive

she no longer ached for a better world
she now understood
that she had been the architect of her story
all along

it was her that was
and always will be
choosing the frequency of her own existence

| TRANSFORMATION

had she not
her life may have looked completely different

conforming
in the lines
mediocre
settled
unchanging
problematic

instead

she chose her own path
and went her own way

| TRANSFORMATION

i'm still growing

into the life
and the person
which and whom
sit patiently within the world
only privy
to my third eye

i haven't yet reached
the destination i 'see'
and deep down i know
that it won't stop there
because 'ever evolving'
is written in my stars

but when i tune in
and notice the changes in me
and the shifts in my world
i know that i am moving towards her
that highest version of self

i stumble often
my harsh inner critic
still booms louder on some days
and questions my direction

but i'm learning to sit with her for a little while
carefully acknowledging and unweaving her concerns
and easing her worries
rather than resisting them

and in the calm, nurturing, joyful nature
which is her
the 'me' existing in realms
i haven't yet explored
patiently awaits 'this me'
to tune back into the vision

i don't know if i will always question life
and my decisions this way
but what i do know
is that it's becoming increasingly easier
to follow my intuition
which in itself is a beautiful thing

and the clarity i have been calling in
is starting to seep through
in magic little moments of presence

| TRANSFORMATION

whatever makes your heart beat
whatever makes you feel alive
go
and
do
that

| TRANSFORMATION

though it was painful
she chose to walk the path

to unlock the chains
one by one
that surrounded her heart

she knew she wanted to show love
and receive that love from others
but the walls she had built were high

still
she chiseled
she knew the pain would be worth the freedom

and as she began to have glimpses of a free heart
she wanted to bring her sisters with her

so she spoke
for all the sisters whose voices shook
she spoke
she believed she could
for all the sisters who were told they couldn't
she believed she could

she endured the pain
so that all the sisters could rise
she endured the pain

for those that came before her
and for those that would come after
she stepped into the fire

she took the blows
she fell
she dived
she felt as though she might drown
but then
miraculously
she took a breath

she climbed
she kept showing up
she let natures energy nurture her
and she rose
she rose above it all
she was free

but more importantly

THEY ALL were free

| TRANSFORMATION

your dreams don't have to change the world
just your world
to one that feels
exactly right
for YOU

| TRANSFORMATION

remember those choose your own adventure books

life is basically that

every choice
will eventually lead us
to the same destination

but it's completely our choice

how much fun we want to have
along the way

| TRANSFORMATION

when you start to do the things
that make you feel good
and start to live in alignment
with who you really are
you will start to notice
subtle synchronicities
showing up in your life

keep going

| TRANSFORMATION

the world told me
who i should be
and what i should say
and what i should do
and how i should act

toe the line and don't make a fuss
it said

i left that world
the one that said my voice didn't matter
i built a new one
with walls of love
and no ceilings

i married a man
he observed my phoenix rising
he didn't say hide her away
he said
without words
okay, be wild
i've got you
i'll hold you
til the end

we had three children
they're magic
we didn't tell them to follow the crowd
we said
without words
do it your own damn way
we've got you
we'll hold you
as long as you need

they never knew of a world
where their voices didn't matter

because we'd already grown our wings
and flown away

| TRANSFORMATION

the outside world can be tweaked
to create balance
but it won't last forever

it's our internal world
that matters most
that's where everlasting change is formed

| TRANSFORMATION

i'm not sure what day it is
and time often eludes me
is it october still

i'll probably forget your birthday
and i probably won't buy you a present
but i promise when i see you in the flesh
i will give you my full presence
and share a meaningful experience with you
that we'll remember forever

i probably won't answer my phone
and i might not call you back until 3 days later but when i do
i will listen intently
to everything you have to say

you might have to get to know me again
because i'm not the same person i used to be
but i'm sure you're not either
and i'd love to know you again too

i don't want to talk about the past
or about other people's lives
i want to know your dreams
and what breaks your heart

i want to hear your story
and the future you yearn for
i want you to tell me about your children
and the quirks they have
that make you love them so hard

i want to see your smile
hear your laughter
allow you to cry
i want to hear your truth,

once upon a time
there were no calendars
no clocks
no pressure to be somewhere all of the time
people came together around campfires
to dance, to sing, to share stories

i feel like I've re-entered that world
no longer wondering
if i was born into the wrong era

i often look like I'm lost
but actually
may just be in the process
of becoming the most found i've ever been

| TRANSFORMATION

take a minute for the really important stuff
everything else can wait

that's you by the way

YOU are the really important stuff

| TRANSFORMATION

hush your inner critic
and allow yourself to shine
beyond
your insecurities

gift yourself the 'knowing'
that you deserve to take up space
too, also, as well
included

lay down your armor
and chip away
at all the walls you've built
peeling
off
thick
skins
and leaving them at the door

dropping into truth

allow me to hold space for your sensitive heart
to see you and hear you and hold you
to HOLD your sensitivity
with gentle hands

until your eyes can see what my eyes see
that this is your gift
not your burden

let us co-create the future
that we know is possible
nurture the reason
that we hold onto hope

here

pain and joy and rage
and everything in between
is accepted
and alchemized
into something beautiful

here

is a place where ego's step aside
so that the soul can dance
where words heal
where love enters
and insecurities die

here

is home
for the sensitive hearts

| TRANSFORMATION

stepping out of our comfort zone
may just open the door
to
a
whole
new
world

| TRANSFORMATION

heal
i heard

because your healing
will help
to heal the world

so i wandered within
to the depths of my broken parts
and felt the pain i had never paused long enough to feel

i located the sadness
that lay dormant
beneath a wall of anger and frustration

life changed
truths became unearthed
i felt a wellness simmering under the surface
snippets of the way it should be;
the way it should feel

but still, the tiredness returned
the dizziness of a world spinning out of control
the ever nagging feeling
that something isn't right

and in a stillness that sunk me into a sadness
that felt almost euphoric
i realized my connectedness with the one
mother earth
woman
i AM her
and this tiredness that i feel in my bones
the feeling of spinning recklessly out of control
the grief
and the sadness
that comes hand in hand with the knowingness
that something isn't right
is because
i AM her

and she is me

and that stillness whispered softly in my ear
listen carefully
the people must come together
to heal the earth first
when she is strong
and vibrant
and joyous
all of us are too
because
we
are
her

| TRANSFORMATION

completely okay
with exactly what is
and open to the magic
of whatever comes next

| TRANSFORMATION

the world might burn
the aliens might come
and none of it has anything to do
with right now's moment

when we fear the future
we miss the point

what we can control
is the moment we are in
right now
and what happens
when we pledge alliance to that

the world changes
our world changes
that's how we change the world

there's so much more to see
if we just open our eyes
to the grass, to the mountains, to the sky

if we take off our far sighted glasses
because they're not doing us any favours

there's no need to look for more
than what is right in front of us
right now
and just be here with that

can we
can I
can you

just be here

with that

        find the others and go dance with them
        outside of the realm you've always known

Section 2

this crazy beautiful trip [that is]

MOTHERHOOD

| MOTHERHOOD

i struggled to express
in just one
small post
a baby announcement that expressed
the essence of my feelings

how does one express so much emotion
in just a few short words
how do you just exclaim
"we're having a baby"
when there's so much more depth to those words

the array of emotions you've felt
and how you've transformed
in those first few weeks
i didn't want all of that
to just be lost
you know

i've always known
this little one
would join us eventually
i did my best to resist because fear
but who am I to stand in the way
of what the universe has planned

albeit the fact
that we're a little scared shitless
i have never actually felt more right
about anything
in my life

it's amazing how our dreams manifest
in the most unexpected ways

i knew we were heading somewhere
i knew it was the right direction
but never would I have guessed that this
was the destination
completely and miraculously
perfect

welcome baby
i've seen you
i've sensed you
you've even already told me your name

and now you're real
you have fingers and toes
and a tiny beating heart
another tiny teacher ready to appear

| MOTHERHOOD

what I'm slowly
but surely
learning
is

it's
perfectly okay
not to be
perfect

| MOTHERHOOD

i cringed when the words
i'm just a mum
would roll off my tongue
i knew what i should have been saying is

motherhood is the most prosperous thing in my world

because it is

| MOTHERHOOD

if sometimes you feel like your kids
are the only ones that don't listen
they're not
if sometimes you feel like your kids
are the only ones who hate bedtime
they're not
if sometimes you feel like your kids
are the only ones who fight
they're not
if sometimes you feel like your kids
are the only ones who say mean things
they're not

and you know what

i would kill to have their energy
and sometimes i don't listen
and sometimes i hate bedtime
and sometimes i fight with my brother
and sometimes i say mean things

because i'm human
and so are my kids

let go of that need to control
let go of the expectation of perfection
let go of the idea that everyone else
knows what they're doing

because they don't

from one sleep deprived mother to another
we're all learning
we're all stuffing it up at times
and we are all in this together

and if any mum tells you differently
then you probably need to give her a big hug
because she's probably the one
that needs it the most

| MOTHERHOOD

sometimes
i wake up
on saturday morning
wanting to flee the building
to refill my cup
and sometimes
that's what i do

but sometimes
self care for me
also just looks like

baking banana muffins
sipping on coffee
and dancing
to a wild woman playlist
in the kitchen
and just like that
i love everyone again

| MOTHERHOOD

stumbled right in
to the most unexpected
and glorious love story
imaginable

being their mum

| MOTHERHOOD

i share my words
so that as you grow
you can look back on this and see
that i didn't always get it right

i was always learning
always growing
always evolving
and i wasn't in any way
shape or form
perfect

i share my words
so that one day
when you have children of your own
and the hard times come
you'll know it was hard for me too
and during the times you get mad at me
for the things i got wrong
you will see
that i was always coming from a place of love

you will see that i am
i always have been
and i always will be
imperfect

and that's okay
because it means
that you can be okay
with who you are too
whatever that might be
and however that might change

most importantly
you will know
how loved you are
in this moment
and every moment to follow

| MOTHERHOOD

the chapters of life
just keep on rolling

note to self;

slow down

and enjoy every moment

| MOTHERHOOD

it's one of those days
when everywhere i look
i see the dirt in my house
and blame myself
for not being better at cleaning

it's one of those days
that i need to go and get groceries
but i can't find one piece of clothing
that looks nice and i can't even bare
to look at my hair and face in the mirror
and i blame myself
for not taking better care of me

it's one of those days
where i don't feel like talking to anyone
so the kids are getting the worst of me
and i blame myself
for not being a better mum

it's one of those days
that i think about all the things
i don't get done
because i don't have enough

arms
legs
time
or energy
and i blame myself
for all of it

it's one of those days
i just want to cry or scream or run away
or just lay face down on my pillow
until the sun comes up again

some days are just really shitty
other days are amazing
today is shitty

i know all these things will get done
i know my mind is playing tricks on me
and i know that these feelings will pass
because tomorrow is a new day

and when I somehow find myself immersed
in a sleeping sandwich with my littlest loves
I realise there's actually no other place
I would rather be

| MOTHERHOOD

always remember
the space between

that empty space

between

each chore
each thought
each breath

that empty space

inside you

that's always at peace
and always there
for you to check in with

| MOTHERHOOD

as i was fumbling in the pouring rain
this morning
with three kids
a hole in my pants
and two shitty umbrellas
that kept turning inside out
i thought
i wish someone would take a photo of this right now
so i can share it
because we all have these moments
even the people we think have it all together
all of the time
have these moments
life is so much more than the still images
that it's portrayed to be
in this day and age
let's not forget that
and let's enjoy all of it
because it's all magic
and to laugh at ourselves in the moments
where everything is a chaotic mess might just be
the most helpful thing
that we can do for another

| MOTHERHOOD

i often make them all stop
and just appreciate
the beauty

the sky
the clouds
the flowers

whatever it may be

they think i'm annoying
but if it's the one thing they carry forward
i'll be happy

| MOTHERHOOD

you've let me know it's time
to come and collect you
and bring you into
this time and space
we'll make this journey
together
a few intense hours
just the two of us
travelling between dimensions
time enough for a connected experience
but not too timely
to exhaust us both
dimmed lights, soft music, oils diffusing
i enter a meditative state
leaving my body to go find you in the ether
and together we return
bliss, connection, euphoria on first sight
the energy in the room is like ecstasy
but still so calm
your birth was divine
you were always coming
welcome to this place sweet soul
enjoy your journey
may I be all that you need me to be
love, your mama

| MOTHERHOOD

i see you out there
breaking cycles
taking responsibility
and changing your story
i recognise you by the way you interact with your children
the pause you take before you react
or the apology you make when the pause doesn't come
and the questions you ask
so that you can understand yourself
or your child more deeply

it's a constant dance
between letting go of the old
and consciously choosing what to bring in next
it's not always easy
and not every day goes the way we would like
but i've found that the key to all of this
is connection to self

you've probably noticed this too
that the more you take care of yourself
the better you feel
and the easier life just flows

Section 3

SONS & DAUGHTERS

this incredible journey, with them

i say 'capturing it all'
but really
i capture so little
i don't catch those moments
when your deep, hypnotic eyes light up
as you share some wisdom with me;
or when you both belly laugh at something
that the other one has said;
or when your blinks start to get longer and longer
as you drift off into dreamland;
and when you fall asleep apart
but he always finds your hand to comfort him

i write it down, because if I didn't
maybe you would never get to know the bond that you both shared
in this here and now;
because it's so easy to forget each moment
as each new one arises

she's quirky
she's sensitive
she's loud
she's free
she's goofy
she's brilliant
she's funny
she's classic
she shines

and each time the world asks her
to be a little less her
to be normal, to be quiet, to be dull, to be small;
i'll be there whispering to her quietly
you girl, are fire
and have been since the day you were born

an inquisitive, curious,
exquisite, gorgeous,
authentic collection of stardust
in the shape of a boy

forever reminding us of what it means to be human
and always teaching us
about the magical essence of life

| SONS & DAUGHTERS

she flies around
and does her thing
sprinkling happiness
wherever she goes

| SONS & DAUGHTERS

he's unlike any human I've met before
but possibly [or definitely]
very much like me
getting to know him
has allowed me to get to know myself
light and shade
this is the crazy, beautiful dance
of parenthood

she is the epitome of being human
she connects, she loves, she feels joy
she is joy

she exudes confidence, she shimmers
and she shines

she is every part of me that has been hidden

i will forego expecting her to grow into someone like me,
and instead,
i will learn to grow in all the ways that will return me to her

may i let go of the resistance
and find the courage
to allow her to always be herself in this world
and allow her to
keep
on
walking
me
home

| SONS & DAUGHTERS

they are living proof
that intelligence and age
have nothing to do with the other

| SONS & DAUGHTERS

i'm learning to take a step back
to let you lead the way
let you follow your own path
and choose the next best step to take
for you
i will always be right here behind you
softly guiding you
in whatever direction you decide to go
but may you learn to trust in your own knowing
of what's right for you
only you can know what's best for you
and if that's the only thing i get to teach you
in this lifetime
that will be enough

| SONS & DAUGHTERS

i'm not sure
i've ever met
a more gentle human heart
than his

| SONS & DAUGHTERS

a message for my daughter's

i want you to know i'd do anything for you
but i also want you to know
that you're capable of doing hard things on your own

i want you to know that sometimes life is amazing
but i also want you to know
that sometimes it's not, and that's okay

i want you to know that the world will ask a lot of you
and that giving is so noble
but i also want you to know
that receiving is equally important

i want you to know that i will always want what's best for you
but i also want you to know
that only you can decide what that is

i want you to know that happiness is your birthright
but i also want you to know
that it's okay to be sad sometimes too

i want you to know that the world will ask you to shrink
to fit into what makes other people comfortable
but i also want you to know
that when this happens you can politely tell the world
to f#ck off

i want you to know that you will always be loved
but i also hope that you will love yourself
always
and first

i want to tell you that i'm not perfect
because i want you to know
that being perfect is not something to reach for

being you is

always be you

because who YOU are

is a gift to this world

she totally messes with my social awkwardness
talks to EVERYONE
steals their rainbow colored dogs
and just generally partakes in life like a little firecracker

where did she come from
i just stand in the background like
yeah
somehow
she is mine

| SONS & DAUGHTERS

a little boy sent here to shift our paradigm

every challenge he gifted us with
has been an opportunity to understand him more
understand ourselves more
and understand life more

he has grown us into better humans who care deeply
about the world we will leave for him

every tantrum he threw
every boundary he pushed
every emotion he evoked in us
pushed us
to learn how to respond
to every challenge in life
with more ease and flow
and more love

lessons that have changed our world
and i know
is just the tip of the iceberg
of the things he will do
he will only continue to make this world better
just by being in it

and i will be his biggest cheerleader
every step of the way

i remember the day you were born
you entered the world so calmly
taking a while to cry
i'd never seen anything more beautiful in my life
and you always kept
that calmness and placidness about you
like you've always known your place in the world
and who you are
so confident in your own skin
with such an infectious energy
people love to be around you

at two, you handed the spotlight over to your brother with such grace
as he demanded my attention
and I fumbled my way through life
as a mum of two

thank you for being so patient
and loving me always
even when i wasn't very loveable

you have taught me so much in four short years
and i know you will continue
to enlighten me so much more
my teacher
my spiritual companion
my reason for wanting to be better

may you always feel safe, happy and loved in this world
and may i always find the strength
to remember
that nothing is more important
than nurturing and guiding
your sacred, gentle, pure, little
heart and soul

glimpsing the secrets of the universe
through her gaze

pure green eyes like the trees
deep brown hair like the dirt
you ground me
i feel your need for stillness
for centredness
for anchoring into this moment
i'm listening
i'm learning
i'm putting you first
the noise around us is loud
but i trust in you
above all else
we are one but we are also separate
you are part of me but you are also you
you bring me back to wholeness
so that you may remain whole too
i surround you in light as i do this work
may what is mine remain mine
and may you always, stay free

| SONS & DAUGHTERS

on one hand
there's a budding little lady
growing up at turbo speed before my eyes

on the other hand
there's just a confused mama
wondering where those four years went
and trying to wind back the clock
while simultaneously
just wanting to see
what each new day will bring

5 years ago you came crashing into this world
with an intense energy that has never left you
you were here for a reason
that's for certain

to push us all out of our comfort zone
and into our authenticity
there was always a strong knowing
that you were calling us to create
a high vibrational environment
where you [and all of us] would thrive

and here you are
absolutely thriving

words will never be enough to describe
how my heart feels about you

i love you
with every cell in my body

the words i speak to her today
will be what she comes to believe about herself

and what she believes about herself
is what she will become

so i'll tell her she's the whole universe
i'll tell her she's limitless
i'll tell her she's free
i'll tell her she can be or do
whatever she chooses
i'll tell her there are no boundaries

i'll tell her she is love
and where there is love
there can be no fear

whatever she dares to dream
can be hers

| SONS & DAUGHTERS

to rest and take time for yourself
can feel so 'wrong' in a world
where being busy is so glorified

but then I come back to my children
what do I want to teach them

and that is enough
for me to honor my choices
and to live a life
that is
first and foremost
completely in alignment
with my own heart and soul

things I want my girls to know
taught by the moon

honor your cycle

remember that it's the darkness
that allows you to shine

acknowledge your stand alone brilliance

and surrender to the phases of life

| SONS & DAUGHTERS

when he's still
he remembers who he is
and the magic in his imagination
will move mountains
he will shape the new world

| SONS & DAUGHTERS

she pulls the threads
i unravel
endlessly grateful it's her

| SONS & DAUGHTERS

if anything can save
this sometimes unkind
world
from itself

it's that same kindness
and love
that you will find in the heart
of my 3 year old son

the children of the new earth
are wiser
more magical
and so beyond our 3D reality
that our imagination
could not even fathom
the beauty that awaits

they are holding our hand
and showing us the way
trust them
tune in
and allow them to lead

Section 4

PARENTING

these moments
this place we call home
their tiny hands in mine

| PARENTING

what if the most important work we will do
in this lifetime
is inside the structure that we call home

what if while we're 'out there'
searching for our purpose
we slowed down and found it
right under our nose

what if our most sacred creation
was building a family unit
that is individual to us

what if we did things our own way
without worrying about what society
or other people
think of us

what if this meant that each member of our family felt free to be
exactly who they are

what if that's how we changed the world

| PARENTING

currently creating : the energy of the container
that holds our family

nothing external even comes close
to being of more importance than this

get the energy right, and everything else
either falls into place
or falls away

we are creating all of it

shout out to all the folks doing the messy but magical internal work

it's a hard slog
but I see you

| PARENTING

will you ever know the extent
of the magic you behold
yeah you will
cos i'll keep telling you
EVERY.SINGLE.DAY
for the rest of my life

| PARENTING

there's a quote about how a mother
will always give up the last piece of pie
for her children

tonight when my husband saw me give my
glass of water to my daughter
i watched as he pushed his water
across the table to me

when you have someone who is willing
to give up what's theirs
because you have given up what's yours
it makes everything just that little bit easier

one life
our way

why: to build a connected relationship with my children and teach them to be connected to all that is

why: so they never have to feel alone

why: so they know that they belong and they know how powerful they are

why: so they are free to be who they are

why: because we all deserve to know that we can smash through glass ceilings

why: to make the world a better place

why: because happiness is our birthright

why: because, freedom

| PARENTING

our first date night in forever
we drove around for an hour trying to decide
then had nandos
can't even deal with how romantic we are

| PARENTING

here's what i know to be true

taking action is the hardest part
but also the most important

our kids thrive when we are thriving

most of the worries we have are from a place far into the future

be.here.now. and make a decision from that place

usually taking the first step is what opens the next door

you are brave enough to step into the unknown

| PARENTING

our children

forever reminding us

that magic is real

| PARENTING

the only way
to encourage our kids
to live their best life possible
and be the best version of themselves
is to live our best life possible
and be our best self

they're always watching us
with eager eyes

| PARENTING

we don't get to hang out much anymore
just the two of us
there's usually at least one little person
searching for our attention
our conversations are often interrupted
by loud screams
and we often feel unheard and forgotten by the other
we struggle to fit each other in
to this new world
that is parenting

but underneath all that
when we take time away from the fast pace
to get in touch with the stillness
where the truth is
what i'm most proud of
is the awareness that we've fostered
together
which has made us a pretty good team
we are learning to give each other space when our moods are low
and not take it personally
we call each other out on our unconscious behaviours
and we voice what we need to say
without fear of judgement

we understand that this part of life

is gunna be chaotic
it's gunna be challenging
it's gunna be messy
it's going to test us
[and above all, we're gunna miss it once it's gone]

so instead of resisting
we must choose to embrace it

sometimes we argue
sometimes our parenting skills suck
sometimes we wonder if we are growing apart
and that's okay

nothing is perfect except accepting imperfection
life is up and life is down
and i'm just glad that I'm on this rollercoaster
with you

even though everything has changed
even though it's different
even though we miss the old us
i think we're growing to love this new us
so much more

especially the new ideas that emerge
in the small pockets of time
we find
to discuss our dreams

dreams of what we will create together
that are so jam packed full of love
because we now understand
that what will fulfill us the most in life
is doing what we can to make this world
a little bit better
for the ones who drive us to an inch of insanity
but at the same time
teach us all about life

| PARENTING

home is

wherever my bunch of crazies are

| PARENTING

our children are here to teach us
that the best version of ourselves
is in reach
and they become our inspiration
and our reason
to reach it

| PARENTING

before you
who was i

a people pleaser
climbing ladders
following crowds
asleep

you woke me up
thank you

| PARENTING

life with little ones
now i don't even bat an eyelid
when my husband asks
"why is there a fork on the cat"

| PARENTING

as we start packing up our house
they start playing together to build their own

a glimpse into our future, perhaps
i do wonder how the story will go
when i tell them of this chapter in years to come

the chapter that held the very individual
yet also intertwined transformations
of me and their dad

from just a girl/boy love story
to the becoming of our family
sure that's easy enough to say
but it's the 'becoming'
that holds the true essence of the story

twas the chapter where
the rediscovering of ourselves began
and our true dreams surfaced
because when we thought we had reached
our ultimate goal
we kept on pondering
kept on wondering what else we might find
if we swayed off track a little

and so

we decided to manaouvre

we gave the conventional life a good crack
but decided to take a leap of faith
and follow our hearts instead
because if that's not the point of this life
then i really can't figure out what is

so we take one step at a time
as the right path continues unfolding in front of our feet
more life. less stuff
more living. less stress
more simplicity. less clutter
more just being, out in the world
with the ones who matter most
them
what that looks like we shall see

just a short time ago making such a huge change felt all too hard
i never believed we would get to this point
living our life basing our decisions on which one feels right
rather than which one looks right
i never thought we would be so brave
but alas, here we are
and off we fly
deep into the unknown

| PARENTING

i get to be right here
watching you
discover this world
and there's nowhere else i'd rather be

Section 5

LOVE

that afternoon
they decided to leave all the worries
of the world
behind
as they drove off
into the sunset
together

| LOVE

it was an extraordinary kind of love
found in the monotony and the mundane
of a story a million times told

found in the day to day of unchanging motion
often buried beneath laundry piles and the like
buried
but never gone

no, it was there

it was there in the visions of the future
in the relentless fight for freedom
and in the breaking of the shackles
from aches and pains of the past

it was there

in the desire for creation
and in the eyes of the children
who found peace in their calm

it was an extraordinary kind of love

the kind that moved through
the battlefield of unconsciousness
and into the brightness of healing

not always an easy love
but a worth it love

and a love they sat and spoke of 50 years later
on the rocking chairs of their porch

it was an extraordinary kind of love

and one they simply titled

us

| LOVE

i'm not here merely to exist
so take me to the places
where life collides with magic
leap
from the edge of comfort with me
let's dive
through the stars
and into the deep blue waters of existence
where your eyes and your smile
are my only compass
into the unknown
the unmapped road we will travel
always lost
yet deeply found

| LOVE

it's in the words of the song your mama would sing
that you'll remember forever

and it's in the rhythmic heartbeat of your dad's chest
that would soothe you to sleep

it's in the heartbreak of being dumped by your first crush

and it's in the reassuring smile
from the quietest kid in the room at that exact moment

it's in being broken by those close to you
and it's in being picked up by the angels
you didn't know surrounded you

it's in the moment your baby is rested on your chest
and it's in the tear falling from her dad's eye
when he looks at you both

it's in the moments you can find peace within your own body
and it's in the moment you can transfer that peace to someone else

it's in the moment that a spontaneous family dance party breaks out
and it's in the moment you apologise to someone you love

it's in the moment you realise that you're no different
to the people who inspire you

and it's in the bravery it takes to begin your own sacred journey

it's in the moment your son looks at you like the world
would stop spinning
if you left it

and it's in the moments that you teach your daughters to always
be as fierce as the world calls for them to be

love is in the lessons we learn from every breath we take
and every moment we get

it's in the places that we want to go
the places we don't want to go
and the places we haven't yet dreamt possible

| LOVE

right now
it kind of feels like we're blowing in the wind
and amidst everything i don't know
one thing i do know for sure
is that i like this direction
let's keep going

Section 6

SIMPLE BEAUTY

take me to a world where there are no rules
and we don't need shoes

| SIMPLE BEAUTY

words can't begin to tell the story of tonight's sunset

| SIMPLE BEAUTY

a note to my niece
sweet frankie girl

i met you in the dream realm
right before you made your journey earthside

i can't wait to hold your tiny hand
in this time and space too

we've got so much to talk about

| SIMPLE BEAUTY

do you ever
just look at the moon
and remember
the magic
of who you are

| SIMPLE BEAUTY

i think children and the older generations
get along so well
because they both know the importance
of the present moment

we remember

then we forget

then we remember again

we remember that time is just an illusion
and that this moment
is all we will ever have

| SIMPLE BEAUTY

counting blessings
setting intentions
and letting
the
waves
wash everything else
away

| SIMPLE BEAUTY

most
of
the
best
moments
come
from
surrendering
into
nothingness

sometimes you meet a friend
and straight away
they feel familiar
as if you've known them at another time
in another world;
and somehow
you find them again
this time around

something deep within you
recognises
something deep within them
and says
oh hey, there you are
i've been looking for you

and then you remain connected
by an invisible string
from one heart to another
no matter where in the world you are

| SIMPLE BEAUTY

i've always been one of those
'depends on the weather' type of people
staying inside if it looks like rain
avoiding places if it's going to be too hot

until recently

when i realised how ridiculous that is

and how much fun i've probably missed out on because of it

so now

who's coming to dance in the rain

| SIMPLE BEAUTY

what a process it's been
nurturing these sunflowers
and now seeing them finally bloom

at one point the stem of one of them snapped
but when it kept on growing
and was the first to bloom
i found great wisdom in it's story

the one that seemed to be broken
courageously kept on growing
and there was a special kind of beauty
that radiated
from that kind of strength

| SIMPLE BEAUTY

there's something special
hidden in each sunset and sunrise
the little whisper that you hear
from the silent beauty of the sky

life isn't meant to be a struggle
appreciate what already is
and be open to receiving even more

Section 7

THE PATH TO HERE AND NOW

it starts with a notion
something is wrong

maybe in the way we react to someone
or in the way we're responding to life
the repetition of that recycled thought

something is wrong
something is wrong
something is wrong

over and over again

and so, the search begins
who can fix me, we inquire
like a rat sniffing out the cheese
like mr burns tap, tap tapping his fingertips
scheming and deliberating
reaching, taking, grabbing, needing

suddenly every self-help guru on the internet
seems to have what we are looking for
seems to know what we are thinking
seems to have the answer
to our deepest aspirations
and so we dabble

repeatedly feeling like
THIS is the answer

but as the fractals of the whole
start to reappear
we continuously find ourselves
seeking the next thing
and the next
next

time and time again
we rise and we fall
until we fall all the way to the ground
we're on our knees
AND STILL
we try to find a way out
THE way out
WHICH WAY IS OUT

but there's nowhere else to go
so on our knees, we pray. God, HELP me
and he gently places a situation into our lives
that reaches us

it's finally loud and clear enough
to shake us out of our slumber
the relentless seeking of answers is over
we have surrendered
we stop. we listen. we look
and we allow those parts of us
labelled "wrong"
to surface

we invite them in
perfection crumbles
oh, i'm the ass hole - that is part of me
the rage, the anger, the jealousy
the ugliness, the judgement
the power struggles - our shame
all.of.it

all of it
is all of us
and THAT is our wholeness
we never needed fixing
we never needed to keep reaching for the next thing
or maybe we did
maybe that was all part of the path

but the true north
was that final drop to our knees
when we were finally courageous enough to say
i'm sick of this shit
i'm sick of my shit
and to sit in that for as long as it takes
as long as it takes to unequivocally
and unapologetically
accept ourselves exactly as we are
ah, there i am
ah, there you are
there we always were
full circle
whole

THANK YOU

Summer, Steele & Luna
The reason I am who I am.
The reason this book exists.
The only legacy I yearn to leave in this world,
is all three of you knowing that you are loved.
I hope this book reminds you of this through any challenging times.

Ben, my partner in life, the father of my children and my safe space in the world. Thank you for always allowing me to voice every crazy idea I have and thank you for supporting me in everything I do.

Mum, Dad & Paul
The ones that have always been there.
Through the ups and downs we never let go of each others hand.
Proud of us.

Lastly, to the Universe/God/My Muse: thank you for showing up just when I needed you most. Your guidance has illuminated my path in ways I cannot fully express.

Danni Kelly resides on the stunning Sunshine Coast of Australia, where she cherishes the simple pleasures of life with her husband and three vibrant children. Inspired by the beauty around her and the everyday moments of family life, Danni's writing captures the essence of motherhood in a heartfelt way.

Whispers from Within marks her debut as an author, a personal journey expressed through poetic reflections. Currently, Danni is also crafting a delightful children's book, blending her passion for storytelling with her love for nurturing family connection. With a commitment to sharing her experiences, Danni invites readers to join her on this creative journey, celebrating the joys and challenges of parenthood.

@_danni_kelly_

www.ingramcontent.com/pod-product-compliance
Lightning Source LLC
Chambersburg PA
CBHW060612080526
44585CB00013B/787